Little Afeni
and
The Cause for Reparations

Nora 'Inora Kamala' Wittmann & Robert 'Ras Kahleb' Gordon

This book is livicated to the African
ancestors and to the children

Little Afeni and the Cause for Reparations text copyright © Nora Wittmann &
Robert Gordon, 2013
Illustrations copyright © Nora Wittmann, 2014
All rights reserved. No part of this book may be reproduced or transmitted
in any form or by any means, electronic, mechanical, or otherwise,
including photocopying, recording, or by any information storage or
retrieval system, without written permission from the publisher, except in
brief quotations embodied in critical articles and reviews.
For information, address *Power of the TrInIty Publishers*,
Tiefer Graben 8-10/49, A-1010 Vienna, Austria.

Power of the TrInIty, Power of the TrInIty Publishers, Power of the TrInIty Creations and the *Power of the TrInIty* logo, depicting the dreadlocked heads of
a woman, a child, and a man, are trademarks of Nora Wittmann.

Please visit our website at www.poweroftthetrinity.net

Book design by Nora Wittmann

FIRST EDITION PUBLISHED BY POWER OF THE TRINITY PUBLISHERS/
Nora Wittmann 2014.

Books are available at quantity discounts for educational, business or promotional use. Please contact info@poweroftthetrinity.net

ISBN: 978-3-200-03802-8

Praise for LITTLE AFENI

"This illustrated children's book on Reparations is the key that opens the door, to children worldwide, on a hidden topic. The book ventures into uncharted territory to tell this story to children who daily identify with intergalactic action onscreen; but are unaware of how their lives have been affected by a most incredible event - which is beyond their imagination. We see this book inspiring other similar work in various media for children of different ages. The authors are to be congratulated for their foresight, initiative, and courage in beginning to address this need."
- **Keturah Cecilia Babb,** RastafarI Reparations Repatriation Working Group, Barbados

"This valuable children's book packs a lot of history into a readable story. It takes us from a peaceful village in West Africa, through the horror of the transatlantic journey to Jamaica. Its message is that the kidnap and enslavement of *Little Afeni* and millions of others caused damage which her present day descendants still suffer. The story calls for the repair of the damage, for the betterment of all humankind. It should be read by children, black and white, for the history is too little known."
- **Lord Anthony Gifford**, QC, attorney-at-law, legal pioneer for slavery reparations

"Our great brother Malcolm X once said, 'Education is the passport to the future, for tomorrow belongs to those who prepare for it today'. And with this passport, we can overcome all frontiers to freedom... The system in which we live often filters or formats information to its interest, so that our young brothers and sisters of the African continent always remain hung up because they are misinformed about whom they really are... at the expense of a mental alienation creating this gangrene that hinders the unity of people... Through this tool, *Little Afeni and the Cause for Reparations*, destined to our little brothers and sisters, we make a step to a new world where free access to education and affirmation of self will no longer be taboo. That JAH guides and gives the necessary energy so that this stone that has been put can become a fundamental edification for our next generations...
One Love!"
- **Tiwony**, number 1 reggae & ragga artist in France

"If the best way of redressing and making reparations for wrongs that began in our past is to prepare for the future, *Little Afeni and the Cause for Reparations* demonstrates the importance of making that investment in our children and those *beautyful* ones yet to be born, now! By equipping children with knowledge required for living as self-determined agents in the cause of their own emancipation, *Little Afeni* succeeds in an essential self-repair task! If we are truly to effect and secure external and internal reparations, we have to inculcate in the children of the world new ways of thinking, dreaming, being and acting in the world. The importance of this book is that it begins to educate children, their parents and guardians into overstanding where their true inheritance lies. (....) In effect, *Little Afeni* encourages children to see their inheritance holistically, globally and cosmically. Through taking into their consciousness the principles of this book, they will better grasp the nature of their full inheritance, of which they have been denied. For they did not just lose a pay check, but their place and status in the world and upon this earth. They will be left knowing that they are entitled to and must recover their stolen legacy and the true wealth that has been amassed by generations of their family lineages the world over. By illustrating how the descendants of the perpetrators of Afrikan enslavement are still today using the resources that are due as reparations to pollute Asase Yaa (Mother Earth), *Little Afeni* is a mighty tool in the armoury for preparing children, from birth, for the real battles they must fight on this Earth. It calls children and their caretakers to battle not only for Afrika and as Afrikans, but to see those battles in the context of upholding, defending and advancing our common humanity, if any of us or indeed our planet is guaranteed a future.

Little Afeni teaches us all, both children as well as the fearless and unblemished child within, the importance of discovering and fulfilling their mission; which is to be part of the repair of not only themselves and this world; but also to recover all that has been taken from and denied to them; and leave this earth more *beautyful* than what they found it. (...) Truly another masterpiece from Power of the TrInIty Publishers!"

- **Esther Stanford Xosei,** Jurisconsult, Pan-Afrikan Reparations Coalition in Europe (PARCOE)

"*Little Afeni and the Cause for Reparations* is a welcome addition to children's literature. Millions of African children were sold into the transatlantic slave trade and plantation slavery and their story is about our past and present. This is a story about justice and remedying a crime against humanity."
- **Prof. Rupert Lewis**, Professor Emeritus in Political Thought at the University of the West Indies and Garvey scholar

"Inora Kamala Wittmann and Robert 'Ras Kahleb' Gordon take on the courageous task of explaining a painful and complex tale to young people in their story, *Little Afeni and the Cause for Reparations*. With the European Union's and the Obama administration's refusal to include the concepts of Pan-Africanism and Reparations in documents related to the International Decade for People of African Descent 2015-2024, the battle for memory takes center stage.

Driven by the profound understanding that *le droit de mémorie*/the right to memory, is the most nuanced combat faced by African descendants, the authors' multi-generational, Diasporic approach to story-telling confronts the looming possibility that the current generation of activists will grow too old and be made too weary to continue the battle for restitutions. At the same time, we are threatened with the prospect of the next generations of African descendants who might be too young and too uninformed to know what the demands and rationale for reparations are about. By supplementing the existing scholarship, this pioneering effort, its characters, provocative and relatable illustrations, not only explains the nature of the Maafa but encourages our youth to remember it is their responsibility to press on with the struggle for themselves and our progeny."
- **Ms. Dòwòti Désir**, Founder & President of the DDPA Watch Group and author of *Goud kase goud: Conjuring Memory in Spaces of the AfroAtlantic*

"I found this story enthralling and an easy read for children. It illuminates the mind and will take them on a real journey while introducing the concept of reparations and slavery and also the bond with Mama Africa and the longing for repatriation."
- **Sis. Sheba**, Chair of the Nyahbinghi Sisters' Council, St. Lucia

"*Little Afeni and the Cause for Reparations* captures in a very simple but detailed manner the major elements of the history of the Transatlantic slave trade, slavery and its devastating impacts on Africa, Africans and the world and therefore indicating that reparations is a must! As the Caribbean continues its struggle for Reparations by way of a formal intervention from CARICOM through a Regional Reparation Commission and National Reparation Committees, the authors must be congratulated for understanding the importance of sensitising and educating our children and doing so with this beautiful story of *Little Afeni*. We look forward to many more stories."
- **Sis. Zakiyah**, Emancipation Support Committee of Trinidad and Tobago

"Traditions of hidden truth have caused the disease of 'IGNORANCE' which must be erased. The first stage of development of a people is the removal of ignorance. The ointment to heal this disease is 'CULTURE CONSCIOUSNESS' and this is what the work 'LITTLE AFENI AND THE CAUSE FOR REPARATIONS' is all about, awakening the minds of the youths. (...) To the parents, please find the time to go through this work with your children from the very tender age of kindergarden so that the experience can remain with them from this time unto that time when REPATRIATION becomes the order of the day with REPARATIONS."
- **Bongo Wisely Tafari**, Chair of the Caribbean Rastafari Organization (CRO)

The Kidnapping and Journey onto the Ship

Once upon a time, not so long ago, in the town of Ijebu-Ode in West Africa, there lived a little girl named Afeni, or "she who loves the people". Her father Tobi was a counselor of the land and her mother Ife a doctor. When Afeni was not in school or in the courts with her father,...

...she accompanied her mom to collect plants, stones and insects used to make medicines. She enjoyed swimming in the Ijebu rivers and studying the plants growing around the waters with her older brother Kayode, her little sister Monifa and their friends. Life was good for Afeni and her family in the land of Ijebu.

But things were beginning to change. In recent times, there had been awful reports of unimaginable things happening in the lands surrounding Ijebu.

One early morning, Afeni was rudely awakened by loud cries and thunderous explosions. Very soon after, she saw that her house was burning and she heard strange voices hurrying her out. The next moment, she realized that she was being bound and taken up roughly by strangers. Some of them appeared to be white as ghosts. Little Afeni was struggling to get free with all her strength. But the intruders placed a wet cloth over her mouth and nose, and this put her back to sleep.

Upon Afeni's reawakening, night had already fallen. It was the light of torches that made Afeni see that she was on a small boat and that she was far from Ijebu. She wanted to sit up but realized that she was bound by her hands and feet. She also saw that there were more people on the boat, chained just like her.
Of course, all of this frightened Afeni greatly and made her cry out aloud, "where am I??". To Afeni's surprise, she heard her brother Kayode answer, "hush little one, I am here, try to sleep a little more." Kayode was behind her; a woman and another boy were seated in between them.
And it was not long after realizing that her brother was so close to her that Afeni fell asleep again.

Early the next morning a stop was made along the muddy banks of the river. Afeni's wrists were hurting and her agony made her bawl loudly. As if in response to her cry, all of a sudden Afeni's captors were attacked by people who had come to help her and the other captives. These people shot many arrows and threw spears in the direction of the captors, some of whom got badly injured.
But then Afeni heard these peculiar sounds of thunder again. She had heard these terrible noises when she was kidnapped from her home. This time, Afeni saw where the explosions were coming from. They were coming from iron staffs that sparked like fire. Wherever these staffs were aimed, Afeni's liberators fell down wounded.

As fast as they could, the kidnappers jumped back into the canoes, taking off with Afeni and the others.
While afloat on the river again, Afeni's mind journeyed to what she had overheard her parents talk about sometimes recently. They spoke about pale looking foreigners bringing strange weapons to the land and taking away people. She had also heard them speak of the town council debating on trading Ijebu's prisoners to these people for something called "gun".
Kayode had managed to move closer to Afeni on the canoe, comforting her to sleep again. Their forced journey to the coast ended the next morning.

At day break, the canoe landed on a small sandy bay where Afeni saw more very pale people. After being kicked out of the canoe, Afeni and the others were roughly dragged down into a dungeon. The dungeon was dark, hot and stinky. The faces of the many people trapped in it expressed grave agony.
During the long days and nights in the dungeon, Afeni and her brother Kayode heard horrible stories of being brought to very distant lands and being forced to labor hard. To Afeni, this was unheard of and she became even more afraid.

When a slaver ship arrived one evening, all were brought out of the dungeon and forced onto it. Though exhausted, the captives put up a fight because they did not want to be taken away on the ship.

At this moment Afeni knew the horrible stories that she had heard were true. Inside this ship was very scary. Cockroaches were crawling all over the walls.

Before the ship set sail, each person was chained down to a small space in the belly of the ship and there was no room to move around at all. As the ship journeyed away from their land, the people trapped inside cried out desperately.

Not too far from the coast, as Afeni prayed silently to the universe, there was a sudden attack on the ship by an African naval patrol. And this time the liberators came with guns.
This happened just as Kayode and a few young boys had been brought up on deck to fetch water for the others. Naturally, Kayode joined in with the liberators and overpowered the kidnapper next to him.

But the kidnappers had more guns and even canons, and again the Africans could not win the fight. And so her big brother Kayode was killed while trying to set Afeni and the other captives free.

Kayode, or "he who brought joy", increased the realm of the ancestors, while Afeni continued the long and dreadful journey on the ship.

Plantation Slavery in Jamaica

These greedy men plotted to sell her, so they took Afeni to the dirty slave market where she made an attempt to escape.
She ran fast, but her captors caught her and sold her into illegal slavery on a sugar plantation.

Because Afeni was rebellious, she was punished left and right and was often sent to labor in the hot sun with the mule.

While Afeni was suffering, far away in the land of Europe evil kings and queens were planning these awful things that were done to Afeni on the slave plantation. They were very greedy for money and wanted to steal many people from Africa. It was these same criminals who had been behind Afeni's and Kayode's kidnapping. And they were planning to capture many more Africans to put them to work without pay. It was five years that Afeni was kept on their plantation.

Oftentimes, Afeni would think of her parents, Kayode, her little sister and the people of Ijebu. She would think of the magical festivals, the music, the delicious foods and her comfortable home. But presently, Afeni's sleeping place was a hen coop. Her scarce meals were scrap meats from butchered animals seasoned with bitter herbs. When beaten with the horse whip, Afeni's deep scars were treated with hot pepper juice and garlic which hurt her even more.

Overworked and mistreated on the plantation, the time came when Afeni could take suffering no longer. Malnourished and weak, she died while giving birth to a son who one day would become a very special man. Her son's name was Abiye, or "he who is born to live".

With the help of his father who was a Maroon, Abiye escaped the plantation and became a great hero of the free African people in the hills of Jamaica.

These Africans, the Maroons, were not slaves. The Maroons destroyed and burned down many of the plantations to free the people. They had fought the criminal enslavers in Africa and were still fighting them in Jamaica.

And like Afeni, most of all, the Maroons wanted to return to their African homeland.

Afeni's Family Today

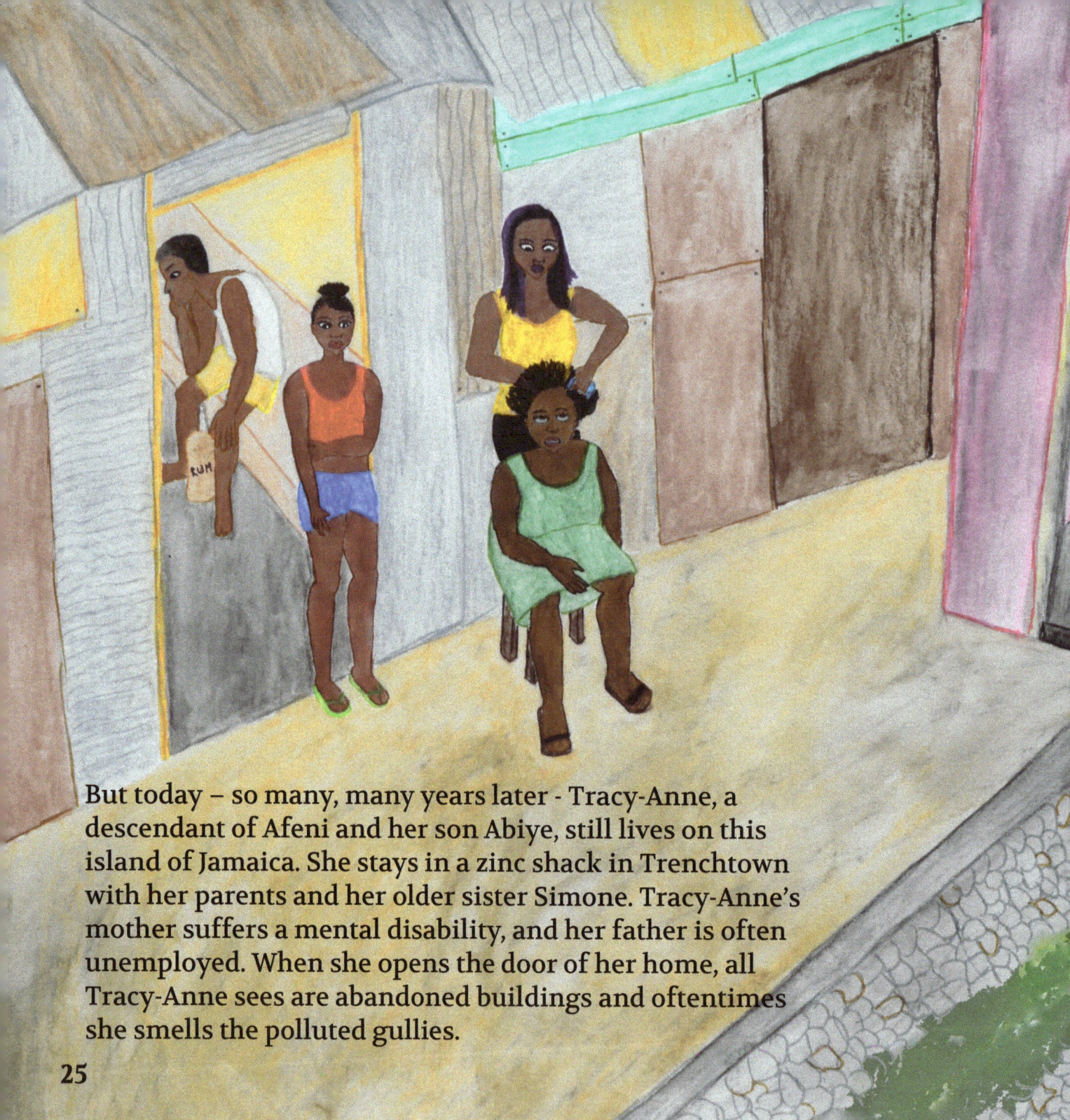

But today – so many, many years later - Tracy-Anne, a descendant of Afeni and her son Abiye, still lives on this island of Jamaica. She stays in a zinc shack in Trenchtown with her parents and her older sister Simone. Tracy-Anne's mother suffers a mental disability, and her father is often unemployed. When she opens the door of her home, all Tracy-Anne sees are abandoned buildings and oftentimes she smells the polluted gullies.

Traditional norms and values known and kept by her ancestors Afeni, Kayode and Abiye have been broken down. Recently, Tracy-Anne has begun to rub a toxic bleaching cream on her face and body. She believes that she will have to look more light-skinned to get a job after leaving school.

Many young people in her community cannot afford to go to school, and they cannot find jobs. Because of this, a lot of violence and crime is happening in Tracy-Anne's community. Sometimes there is so much violence going on all around that children cannot go outside to play.

Tracy-Anne also has a cousin named Iyah. Iyah is a Rasta and teaches mathematics at a high school in Montego Bay, on the other side of the island. Sometimes he is faced with discrimination because of his African identity. Just recently, a group of parents complained about him because he tells the students that mathematics, physics and chemistry originated in Africa.

Meanwhile on the continent of Africa, Sayouba who is a descendant of Afeni's little sister Monifa is not well at all. Two years ago his mother died. His grandmother then came to live with him and his two little brothers. But a few months later, his father became sick and the people started to say that it was AIDS.
In school, Sayouba heard the boys discussing that precious stones and diamonds could be found in a part of the country where a war is raging.

So Sayouba decided to go there and dig for diamonds to help his family. Now he works in a stone-pit guarded by armed men. Sayouba has to pay them to be allowed to search. And afterwards he goes to the office that belongs to a white man to sell his stones.

Since arriving at the mine, Sayouba barely has enough food to survive and he coughs a lot now because of the heavy dust. Once, he tried to search in the quarry without paying the guards. They beat him up so bad that Sayouba could not work for two days. Sayouba is afraid. He asks himself if he ever will be able to return to his family.

Recently, in the time of the rains, Sayouba caught malaria. No one around him has the money to buy the medicines, and no one seems to remember the medicinal plants that could save his life. All of this is because transatlantic slavery destroyed so much knowledge and broke down the security of African people. Like Afeni and Kayode, many Africans were lost on the African continent.

In America, another member of Afeni's family lives in Chicago today, in a housing project known as the Cabrini Green. Tamika is a descendant of Afeni's cousin Ayo who was kidnapped twenty years after Afeni was.

Lately, Tamika has not been sleeping well at all because bulldozers are destroying the buildings of her neighborhood.

She also knows that before their ancestors were kidnapped and enslaved, they were living happy and healthy lives in Africa. That is why Joanne is active in the movement for reparations. The word "reparations" means all actions to repair a damage or harm caused by wrongdoing.

And she and her mother Joanne have nowhere else to go and live, but their home is not the best place to reside either. Not long ago, Tamika fell sick with lead poisoning from drinking the water coming through the old pipes. Nearby, not even a mile from their building, there is a lake so polluted that it is filled with blind and dead fish. Tamika's mother Joanne knows that their awful situation in America is because of the crime of transatlantic slavery and all of what has been taken from their family for such a long time now.

According to the law, the wrongdoers must pay for the repair. But with slavery, there was no repair yet.

The Repair

Though the repair is long overdue, it still remains necessary today for a lot of reasons. Before slavery, Afeni's family had a better quality of life on the African continent than their descendants scattered all over the world have today.
And the law says that when a wrong is done, the wrongdoer must provide the means to repair the situation. Also according to the law, those who were offended have to be given back the quality of life that they would normally fulljoy without the illegal wrongdoing.

And if slavery had not happened, Tracy-Anne, Iyah, Sayouba, Tamika and Joanne would live in Africa today, prosperous and healthy. They would grow their own fresh foods on their own land, receive the best education, and be apppreciated in the community for their work. The descendants of the wrongdoers owe lots of money for the labor that was stolen from Afeni and the other ancestors.

With these monies, Tracy-Anne, Iyah, Sayouba, Tamika and Joanne would go to good schools, eat good foods and have good housing.

Since Tamika and Joanne long for a reunion with their family in Africa, reparations will enable them to go there freely. And to Iyah, who wants to go back to Africa to stay and live, the descendants of the wrongdoers owe the money to rebuild his home there. Yet, Africa also needs repair so that Iyah can fulljoy the high life quality of his ancestor Afeni. Like Little Afeni, so many people were stolen from Africa.

This left many communities impoverished and created a lot of problems. So, reparations deal with repairing the wrongs done to Afeni, her family and all of Africa.

In fact, the entire world is in serious trouble today because of transatlantic slavery. With the monies made from the work of Afeni and millions of Africans, the kidnappers' descendants continue to do so many bad things today. They pollute the rivers, the sea and the air. They destroy the good food and sell the people bad food that makes them sick. The kidnappers' descendants also steal water and minerals from people. They still oppress and hurt people, just like Sayouba in the stone-pit, remember? For all these reasons, reparations for slavery are very important today. The wrongdoers must be stopped NOW!

But those who got rich from illegal transatlantic slavery do not want to repair and give back the money owed....

Thus, Afeni and all the ancestors are counting on YOU, little boys and girls, princes and princesses, to achieve reparations. For this task you need to prepare well. Please become good lawyers and judges, historians, educators, writers, artists, farmers, mathematicians, architects, engineers, chemists, doctors, healers, water experts, archaeologists, and much more.

Little Afeni is your great-great-great-great-great-great-great-great-great-great-great-great-great-great-great-grandmother.
She counts on you to restore and heal Africa. Africa is our future.

Also available from Power of the TrInIty Publishers

books

organic cotton shirts

earrings, etc.

More books coming soon

Watch out for the vegan
"Conscious Around the World Cookbook"©

www.ingramcontent.com/pod-product-compliance
Lightning Source LLC
LaVergne TN
LVHW070058080426
835508LV00032B/3489